Reggie

Wonderful

we will always keep that
wish in our minds and hearts.
All our love, Barb & Graham

The Steps to
Healing

Also by Dana Ullman, M.P.H.

~~~~~~

Books

Homeopathy A–Z

Everybody's Guide to Homeopathic Medicine
(with Stephen Cummings, M.D.)

The Consumer's Guide to Homeopathy

*Homeopathic Medicines for
Children and Infants*

Discovering Homeopathy

Audiocassette

Homeopathic Healing

ରଉ ରଉ

Please visit the Hay House Website at:
www.hayhouse.com

~~~~~~

To those people who take
the steps to healing and
avoid the elevator

~~~~~~

Contents

~~~~~~~~~

Introduction

~~~~~~~~~~

The Doctor Is In

We commonly talk about the *wisdom* of the body, but all too often we don't think about the *humor* of the body. As magnificent as the human body is, it's a bit strange that our feet run and so does our nose, our mouth speaks and our stomach talks back to us, our knees knock and our ears ring. Hopefully, somebody is at home there to respond to of all this commotion.

When you think about it, the body is wonderfully creative in producing whatever symptoms it needs to get our attention. Aching, throbbing, cramping, itching, and inflaming are but some of the special effects it indulges in. It's also fond of sight gags and sound effects: It erupts, discharges, and discolors, and it emits gas and odors that get our attention (as well as that of those around us). It also calls attention to its problems by producing effects that make us feel feverish or fatigued, nauseous or nervous, and stiff or spastic. No bells and whistles, but just about everything else.

Even though there is a wisdom of the body, it isn't always easy to figure it out. What is the logic behind an allergy to cats? Is it some sort of survival mechanism developed to protect us from killer pussycats? Are violent sneezing attacks nature's attempt to blow away the life-threatening felines? Every ailment has its mysteries.

This book will not try to answer *all* of your questions about health, but it will answer *many* of them. It will also provide you with a deeper understanding of the innate healing powers within you, give you some practical insights about the human body, and present you with sound and effective ways to heal your body temple.

This book consists of 22 steps to health, which outline the underlying principles of the healing process. These steps are worth your careful attention—and since health is not a spectator sport, it also requires your participation. Healing is not simply a matter of applying a specific treatment to a specific problem; it is also about deepening your understanding of the human body and of nature, and an ability to use this knowledge to create a more healthy and joyful life. These steps help you see the bigger picture, and they provide insight into why some healing techniques work and others don't, and why it's ultimately the way they are used that influences their effectiveness. However, while these steps to healing are basic and important, they are not the world's *only* healing principles. I hope that each of you will discover and use additional healing practices that work particularly well for you.

Waking Our Inner Doctor

The great physician and humanitarian Albert Schweitzer acknowledged the importance of every body's self-healing capacities when he said, "Each patient carries his own doctor inside him. They come to us not knowing that truth. We are at our best when we give the doctor who resides within each patient a chance to go to work."

The primary purpose of this book is to make you aware of this inner doctor and to offer specific strategies that will let that doctor perform his or her daily miracles. Although there is much that physicians and other health professionals can do to prevent and treat disease, there is much more that each of us can do on our own. Our health is too important to leave to someone else.

All healing is really *self*-healing. The drugs or herbs we take in the treatment of infection may have antibacterial properties, but unless your own immune system is strong enough, true healing does not occur. A surgical procedure or a colonic may remove an unhealthy growth or substance, but unless your own defenses are strong enough to prevent it from coming back, true healing does not take place. Healthy foods and vitamin supplements may provide you with a nutritious diet when you are sick, but unless you have the internal building blocks to make use of these nutrients, true healing will not be the result.

To get healthy, your immune system must

have a certain vigor and spark. Effective atti-
tudes and treatments ultimately catalyze this
spark so that the healing potential within
awakens and spreads. Each step to healing in
this book provides a little more understanding
of your own body's processes. When applied,
each does its part to increase and strengthen
the body's self-healing capacities. Each step
takes you to a higher vantage point in which
you can see the bigger picture and feel greater
levels of health, joy, and love.

It has been said that the best time for
someone to start the healing process is ten
years ago. The second best time is today. If
you're ready to start healing yourself now, this
book will provide the steps to help make that
happen.

The Steps

#1

~~~~~

You Are the Most Important Member of Your Health-Care Team

"The next major advance in the health of the American people will be determined by what the individual is willing to do for himself."
— John Knowles,
former president of the Rockefeller Foundation

According to the rules of the universe, each person is not only required to *play* on their own health-care team, they are required to *manage* the team, too.

To organize your health-care team, it is important to first realize that doctors and other health-care professionals are your employees. That's right—the doctor doesn't pay you; you pay the doctor. The doctor is your expert consultant on medical matters. So, if this employee doesn't complete the job of answering basic questions about your health, he or she should be replaced, even fired.

To paraphrase Bob Dylan, a weatherman doesn't need to tell you which way the wind blows. Likewise, you don't always need a doctor to tell you how to feel better. Although medical care can be invaluable and sometimes crucial, there are many conditions that are more easily treated using simple home remedies, instead of complicated and expensive conventional medical treatment.

Western medicine offers what may be considered as "the Cadillac of medical care." But just as it isn't always necessary or ecologically sound to drive a Cadillac everywhere, it isn't always appropriate to receive this type of medical treatment. Simple home remedies can sometimes provide that extra nudge your body needs, while the big guns of medicine can be saved for more drastic situations.

How you eat, exercise, deal with stress,

and express yourself can both help prevent illness and promote health. This attention to your health does not have to be the chore that some people make it. A healthy lifestyle can be wonderfully invigorating, enlivening, and even joyful, and if it isn't, you're probably doing something wrong.

Determining the healthiest things you can do for yourself usually requires personal study, self-reflection, and expert assistants. Here's where organizing your own health-care team comes in.

People often put more energy into choosing an auto mechanic than they do in selecting their health-care provider. To find a good medical professional, it is necessary to do some homework. Ask your friends or other people you trust which doctors they recommend. Find out if he or she listens, explains things clearly, informs patients of various options available, encourages patient involvement in health, and is knowledgeable about self-care strategies.

In addition to considering the various conventional medical specialties, you should also consider adding to your team an acupuncturist, homeopath, naturopath, chiropractor, psychologist, social worker, religious leader, nutrition-ist, stress management consultant, or exercise coach. This isn't to say that you need to see *all* of these experts. As the manager of this team, you decide who is in the batter's box with you and when.

Whomever you choose, it's important to make sure that they do nothing *to* you, only *with* you. And if they do not directly discuss with you the different ways you can improve your own health, they are not enlisting the help from the most important member of the health-care team—*you!*

There is a tendency to blame the medical professional for not making the patient better. Although this is sometimes true, it's important to remember that every time you point your finger at someone or something else as the source of your problems, you also have three more fingers pointing back at you know who.

෧෧ ෧෧

#2

~~~~~~~~

WHEN NATURE CALLS, ANSWER

"We command nature only by obeying her."
— Francis Bacon

One of the ways that your car tries to warn you of an impending problem is by flashing a warning light at you. A symptom of malfunction in your car is like a symptom in the body; it is trying to tell you something.

When your oil light comes on, do you try to unplug it? Probably not, yet we commonly seek to turn off and suppress our symptoms as our way of dealing with them. However, like the car that has a flashing oil light, unless something is done to deal with the problem, it may get worse.

Quite different from signals in a car or other machines, symptoms of the body do not only indicate that something is wrong, but they are also adaptive responses of the body in its efforts to deal with stress or infection. By turning off this adaptive response, we inhibit our own ability to defend and heal ourselves.

A fever, for instance, is an important defense of the body. It is the way that the body creates an internally heated environment so that viruses and bacteria cannot survive as easily. During a fever, the body's white blood cells become more active, and the body's own antiviral chemical, interferon, is secreted in greater amounts. It is therefore predictable that drugs that suppress fever not only prevent the body from healing, but can also cause serious side effects.

Suppressing a symptom is like shooting a messenger because you don't like the message. The messenger may die, but the message remains the same.

A "symptom" is any phenomenon or circumstance accompanying something and serving as evidence of it. So, when we treat a symptom, we are not necessarily treating the disease that is causing it; we are treating a manifestation of the illness, not the illness itself.

We commonly view symptoms as something wrong with us and develop a mind-set that assumes that we must rid ourselves of this "problem." We then utilize various treatments that seek to eradicate the symptom, inhibit the disease, and attack the problem. We ultimately are trying to control, outwit, and dominate nature. In so doing, we are setting up an adversarial approach to dealing with our affliction.

The common practice of treating a headache with painkillers is a classic example of this adversarial approach. The word *painkiller* alone lets us know that we are trying to attack or kill something, yet the head pain is only a symptom of the disease. Whether the headache results from the stress of a relationship, overwork, a response to overeating, drinking too much coffee, or whatever, treating the head pain with a painkiller does nothing to address the source of the symptom. And to make matters worse, the body now has to deal with a drug that is suppressing the body's effort to call attention to a problem.

The fighting language of conventional drug treatment is distinct from a mind-set that is oriented towards working *with*, instead of *against*, the body's efforts. Instead of turning off symptoms, this gentler mind-set is apt to consider approaches that attempt to strengthen the immune system, augment the person's own defenses, and nurture the body's own healing capacities.

Instead of ignoring our own symptoms or simply letting the doctor figure out what to do, we can use our illness as an opportunity to figure out what our symptoms are saying to us. They may be telling us that something in us is out of balance with our environment or that something in our environment is out of balance with us. Whatever method a person chooses to determine what this something is, illness is an opportunity to seek greater understanding of ourselves and our interaction with the world. Illness is also an opportunity to seek to change ourselves or to work to change our environment.

Of course, many people choose not to try to understand or change anything. It is no wonder that such people often get and keep their chronic illnesses.

The human organism, however, has impressive, even incredible, adaptive healing capacities that have been developed and refined over thousands of years. When we can learn to reestablish a healthy balance between our bodies and the world that surrounds us, the body is better able to work its wonders to heal itself.

We must carefully listen to our own symptoms, as well as to the world in which we live. Robert Frost emphasized the importance of this type of listening when he wrote:

How many times did it thunder before Franklin took the hint?

How many apples fell on Newton's head before he took the hint?

Nature is always hinting at us.

It hints over and over again.

And someday we take the hint.

These words have great meaning for those of us who are seeking to understand the hints that our bodies give us all the time. Do you acknowledge these hints? Do you do something about them? Next time nature calls, be sure to *answer*.

#3

~~~~~~~~~~

YOUR HEADBONE IS
CONNECTED TO YOUR . . .

*"The human body is the best picture
of the human soul."*
— Ludwig Wittgenstein

The mind and the body are undeniably inter-connected. Anyone who doesn't recognize that the mind can readily create physical symptoms is unwittingly cutting off his or her head at the neck. This Marie Antoinette–style of medicine is a tad out of date.

Emotional and mental states have certain effects on the body; likewise, the body has the power to create such states. Just as we probably know of someone who became ill shortly after a crisis in the family, we've probably also heard of someone who suffered from a lengthy or unpleasant illness and later became depressed, anxious, fearful, or a bit crazed as a result.

An integral aspect of Chinese medicine recognizes the connection between organ systems and emotional states. The liver, for instance, is related to anger, the lungs to depression, and the kidneys to fear. Thus, if a person has a diseased liver from drug or alcohol abuse, it is likely that the individual will experience more than a modicum of anger. Even our language, which calls a person "bilious," acknowledges this connection between anger and a person full of bile. Likewise, a person with a lung condition is usually less able to breathe efficiently, often leading him or her to feel more depressed than normal. The simple act of sighing, the effort to take a deeper breath, is intertwined with feelings of sadness. The kidneys, which are situated just below the "fight or flight" adrenal glands, are directly affected by and directly affect the emotion called fear. Chinese medicine readily acknowledges the dynamic interplay between psyche and soma, for they recognize that emotional disturbances are as likely to create physical disorders as physical disturbances are able to create emotional disorders.

It is sometimes useful to know which came first—the psychological problem or the physical one. However, this knowledge is not always obvious, and it isn't always helpful. Just as it is of no value trying to extinguish the original match that set the forest afire, trying to figure out which came first—the chicken or the egg—may not matter much to every farmer or omelet-eater.

In the same way that a fireman must put out the entire blaze, not just the larger flames, the best strategy to deal with a sick individual may be to treat the whole person. Although the term "treating the whole person" has become almost trite these days, it is sometimes worthwhile to use various strategies concurrently, which each attempt to heal one or more of the blazes in the body and the mind. Treating liver problems, for instance, may require reducing drug and alcohol intake, reducing exposure to toxic substances, increasing intake of vitamin

A and green leafy vegetables, starting a relaxation program, and learning to express anger constructively.

Using many healing methods at once is sometimes the best strategy, although another approach is to use a single method that focuses squarely on the primary source of the problem. If a hyper-stressed person who is experiencing headaches greatly benefits from breathing exercises, it may not be important to consider other headache treatment strategies. Applying a specific treatment to what may be the center of the primary irritation may alone create a special peace and a powerful healing.

Making the decision to try one approach or another to deal with your mind and body problem should not be simply a rational decision, but also an intuitive one. In addition to asking your left brain and your right brain to help you figure this out, you might also consider asking your headbone, your neckbone, your shoulderbone . . . it's all connected.

಄಄ ಄಄

#4

~~~~~~

SEEK INNER WISDOM

*"Direct your eye inward and
you'll find a thousand regions in your
mind yet undiscovered."*
— Henry David Thoreau

Psychologist Lawrence LeShan once
remarked, "If the brain were so simple that
we could understand it, we would be so simple
that we couldn't."

Some brain researchers do not think of the
brain so much as an *organ* of perception, but as
a *filter* of perception. The brain, they say,
absorbs much more than we realize. They
crudely estimate that we become aware of only

about 10 to 15 percent of what the brain absorbs. The remaining or hidden information becomes a part of our subconscious mind.

This information may sound great, but what can anyone do with it, and how can anyone get access to that other 85 to 90 percent?

One trick to getting access to the hidden wisdom of the brain is to not try. Researchers have frequently described this Zen paradox. There are innumerable stories of scientists who were working extremely hard on a specific problem for days, weeks, months, or years . . . and then, in an unexpected moment of relaxation, sometimes during sleep, a special insight came to them, thus providing an important piece to the puzzle. For example, there is the story about Albert Einstein, who had been struggling with one of the complex concepts that would lead to his Theory of Relativity. On one particularly beautiful day when he went sailing and was feeling very peaceful and relaxed—voilà—the solution he was searching for came to him without effort.

Even Yoda, the Jedi knight from *Star Wars,* taught Luke Skywalker that to get in touch with "the Force," it was necessary to stop trying.

Another trick to accessing subconscious information is to relax, meditate, and simply but directly ask a question that you want answered. Don't try to answer it yourself; just listen to see if an answer comes to you. This may seem woo-woo to some people, but this process, at worst, gives you an opportunity to be clear on the question you want or need answered, and at best, it may help you tap in to the further reaches of the brain and get access to the information you seek.

This exercise may also be used medically. You can tune in to your "inner doctor" and ask for a diagnosis or advice on what you should do about your condition. This inner doctor may take the form of a person, an animal, or even an object. The information may come in the form of symbolic words, images, or gestures that have a special meaning. It is sometimes difficult to figure out what is being said, and yet, when considering different possible meanings, people often notice that one interpretation feels right.

The inner doctor's suggestions for treatment may be something you can do for yourself, or it may be that you should seek a specific specialist for treatment. People who seek advice from their inner doctor do not always receive recommendations for natural therapies; they may be encouraged to see a physician or even a surgeon. The inner doctor may also suggest that the symptoms are the cure and that the best thing the sick person can do is let the symptoms run their course without impediment.

Being a hard worker, your inner doctor also operates while you sleep, when dreams are the medium of communication. Like other processes that access your subconscious mind, these messages are usually symbolic and require intuition to interpret. In order to prepare yourself for the doctor's advice, consider repeating to yourself just before falling asleep, "I ask for guidance, and I allow you to enter my dreams."

Get in touch with your inner wisdom, for you are smarter than you think.

And after you've gotten comfortable contacting your inner doctor, you can start tuning in to your "inner financial consultant" if you're having money problems. You can also tune in to your "inner coach" if you want to improve your sports performance. And . . . on and on . . .

#5

~~~~~~~

You May Be Responsible for Your Health, but You're Not Always to Blame for Your Disease

*"There are responsible persons,
but there are no guilty ones."*
— Albert Camus

When you hear people say that they're *responsible* for their health and to *blame* for their disease, they are exhibiting a classic form of "wellness macho." This machismo attitude leads people to assume that an individual has much greater power and influence than one actually has.

The assumption behind this belief is that we create our own reality and that we are responsible for whatever infections we have because we allowed ourselves to be infected. We are responsible for whatever chronic diseases we have because we have not done whatever was necessary to strengthen our own immune system. And we are responsible for genetic diseases because our soul picked our own parents before we were born.

The further reaches of this perspective is that people allow drunk drivers to hit them, passengers knowingly choose to board a plane that crashes, and families in Love Canal were responsible for their exposure to environmental toxins. This attitude is not limited to New Age subscribers. Even during the Depression, a large percentage of men blamed themselves for being out of work.

We do indeed cause various problems for ourselves, many more than most of us presently recognize. However, to think or say that we create *everything* is to ignore the obvious and far-reaching influence of our physical and social environment. To assume that each individual creates his or her own fate is to maintain an incredibly egotistical view of the world.

One serious side effect of wellness macho is the feelings of guilt it creates, and the last thing that a sick person needs is this additional emotional weight. To make matters worse, these guilt-ridden people then expend great energy in searching for what they did to "cause" their misfortune, when their energy could be used more effectively if applied to healing.

At the other extreme of placing responsibility for disease are those people who assert that social, political, and environment forces are so strong that they overpower the individual. This extreme position ultimately victimizes individuals and disempowers them by assuming that there is nothing that an individual can do for their own health except to try to change the social, political, and environmental effects upon them.

Whether the notion that we create our own diseases seems perfectly logical or completely preposterous, one value that it holds is that it can help empower us. It reminds us that we have the power to greatly influence our own lives. It encourages us to no longer blame others for our problems. We can find lessons to be learned in everything that happens to us. For instance, if you have weak knees, perhaps you may take this as a sign to stand up for yourself. If you have poor digestion, you simply have to be more conscious of eating healthy foods. If you have a headache, you may realize that you have to relax more often. On a more serious level, if you are paralyzed, you may need to learn how to ask for help from others.

There is indeed something valuable in the assumption that trying to learn from your circumstances is a much more effective strategy than being devastated by them.

Perhaps the best strategy to deal with wellness macho is to recognize the difference between being responsible for your own health and being blameworthy for your illness. Rev. Jesse Jackson shed light on this differentiation when he told a high school audience, "You may or may not be responsible for being *down*, but you *are* responsible for getting *up*." Likewise, you may or may not be responsible for being ill, but you are responsible for *doing* something about it.

ᏰᎧᏰ

#6

~~~~~~~~~

THE TEN STEPS TO
HEALTHY EATING

*"Diets are for people who are
thick and tired of it."*
— Mary Tyler Moore

According to the American government, the Standard American Diet is S.A.D. If "you are what you eat" is true, many Americans are probably Twinkies, Frosted Flakes, and Ding-Dongs. When you consider that the nutrients we ingest today become tomorrow's muscle, nerve, and brain cells, it is frightening to consider what becomes of a person who maintains a steady diet of junk food.

It's no wonder that some people have Twinkie muscles, Frosted nerves, and Ding-Dong brains.

Hippocrates, the Father of Medicine, said, "Let food be your medicine." This doesn't necessarily mean that food is the *only* medicine, but it does emphasize the fact that foods are not only tasty but also nourishing and healing. Bananas, for instance, can help heal ulcers; onions can relieve bronchial congestion; mushrooms can inactivate certain viruses; and cranberries can prevent and cure urinary tract infections.

Although foods have the power to heal, they also have the power to create dis-ease. Milk products, wheat, eggs, and chocolate are common foods that many people are allergic to. Such foods will not only create various digestive problems, but they can also cause various symptoms, including great fatigue, recurrent headaches, and disturbing emotional and mental problems. As the old saying goes, "One man's meat is another man's poison."

Finding the right foods and combinations of foods that are right for you is not always easy. Perhaps this is why a nutritionist friend of mine calls herself an "interior decorator." Although there is little upon which all nutritionists agree, there are some generally recognized steps to healthy eating that, if followed, will be beneficial to your well-being.

1. There is no ideal nutrition program for everyone. Not only does each person have their individual nutritional needs, but these needs can change from season to season and year to year. Where and how people live also influences their nutritional requirements. For example, people in cold climates require more caloric intake and must eat more cooked foods than people in warm climates. The degree of physical activity or emotional stress in a person's life will also affect their nutritional needs. So, too, can genetics play a role in determining nutritional needs, because the body becomes accustomed to what our ancestors ate.

2. The type of food you eat is more important than what vitamins and supplements you take. Many foods not only contain many common nutrients, but also numerous trace elements that are important, even essential, for health. Chromium, boron, molybdenum, vanadium, and manganese are all important in maintaining health, yet they are not commonly in the typical vitamin supplement.

Foods often contain a complement of nutrients that make them easier to digest. Oranges, for instance, not only have vitamin C, but they also have bioflavinoids, which help the body assimilate this vitamin more efficiently. Eating an orange, then, is a more efficient source of getting and assimilating important nutrients than popping a pill.

In addition to the common nutrients, there are other known and unknown vital enzymes and ingredients in fresh foods that are a part of life itself.

3. Eat fresh foods whenever possible. Processing reduces the nutritional content of food. Frozen, canned foods, and prepared foods will not be as nutritious as those that are made from fresh ingredients. Although our fast-paced modern lifestyle encourages a tendency to eat processed food, we often suffer from a health standpoint as a result. Many fresh foods can actually be prepared easily and rapidly. The trick is learning to make quick, natural, and fresh snacks and meals, and you'll be surprised by the amount of foods you can eat and how good they taste.

4. Eat food low on the food chain. Pesticides accumulate in greater concentrations in animals that are higher on the food chain. A vegetarian diet that consists primarily of whole grains, beans, vegetables, and fruits sharply reduces the level of exposure to pesticides and other toxins. Other "side effects" of this diet are reduced rates of heart disease, cancer, and numerous other acute and chronic illnesses. Can you afford not to eat "low" on the food chain?

5. Eat organic foods whenever possible. Eating organic foods will not only reduce your exposure to toxic pesticides, they also tend to have greater nutritional value because they are grown in more fertile soils due to the use of organic fertilizers. Although it is still uncertain how much pesticide one must ingest to disturb the bodily functions or cause illness, it is certainly wise to limit exposure to it.

When possible, it is worthwhile to find out if the foods you are buying come from the U.S. or another country. Many pesticides that are banned in this country come back to us in imported food. This is but one more example of karma playing out its drama.

Organic foods are often significantly more expensive than non-organic foods, although this price difference is diminishing as demand for these safer foods increases. In the meantime, the extra cost for organic foods is worth the peace of mind and body that they give. The additional benefit of eating organic foods is that you are reducing the use of pesticides in the environment and therefore helping to creating a healthier planet. Buying organic foods also supports the organic foods movement and industry and puts your money where your mouth, stomach, and health should be.

6. The hunger reflex means that you should eat. As simple as this may sound, many people eat whether they are hungry or not. Evolution has endowed our body with a sophisticated method of knowing when to eat.

Some people are very hungry in the morning, others are not. Some people more efficiently digest food when they eat frequent small meals, and tend to get sleepy after a large lunch or dinner.

Knowing when to stop eating is as important as when to start. Malnutrition is not simply a condition of not having enough to eat; it is also a condition in which a person has too *much* to eat. It may be strange to call some obese people "malnourished," but technically, it's true. It is most healthful to err by undereating rather than overeating. Recent research has suggested that animals who were slightly underfed lived considerably longer than those who were overfed.

7. Chew your food. Each stage of digestion is dependent upon the previous stage, and the first stage of digestion is proper chewing. During this mastication, you are not only breaking down the food so that it can more easily slide down your throat, you are saturating the food with important salivary enzymes that begin the digestive process. Chewing carbohydrates is particularly important because salivary enzymes help to digest them. Too-rapid swallowing of carbohydrates means that the pancreas is forced to bear the extra burden of digesting them, and considering most people's sugar-laden diets, the pancreas is already overworked.

Some nutrition zealots recommend chewing food until it is liquid in the mouth. They even say you should chew your drinks. While these are worthy goals, you needn't get too crazy doing so. Still, when you ultimately think about it, if you don't chew your food, who will?

8. You are not what you eat; you are what you assimilate. Because we do not assimilate all the nutrients from the food we eat, it may be more apt to say that we are what we assimilate, or more crudely, we are what we don't poop.

Even the healthiest people do not absorb all the nutrients they ingest. People with digestive disturbances or with food allergies are even less able to fully absorb the food they eat. Although research on this subject is still relatively limited, it is known that certain nutrients make absorption of other nutrients more difficult, while others make it easier. For instance, numerous foods and drinks inhibit calcium absorption, including grains, spinach, chard, rhubarb, chocolate, peanuts, walnuts, soybeans, alcohol, and caffeine. Foods that aid calcium absorption include citrus fruits, apples, broccoli, carrots, cabbage, tomatoes, onions, cauliflower, and dark green leafy vegetables.

9. Emotional states can disturb digestive function. Various emotional states can inhibit digestive juices and stifle the digestive process. If you are having an argument during a meal, poor digestion is almost inevitable. If you think that the food you are eating isn't good for you, your anxiety may make it true. If you are eating while feeling depressed, expect your digestion to be depressed as well; and to make things worse, this slowed-down digestion may lead to unwanted weight gain.

Because we "season" our food with our thoughts and emotions every time we eat, next time you're at the dinner table, don't ask anyone to pass the guilt, fear, anxiety, or anger.

Such emotions can disturb digestion and do not combine well with any foods. It is healthier and wiser to bless the food, bless the people with whom you are eating, and bless yourself. This is a healthy combination that best helps assimilate food for the body, mind, and soul.

10. Eat foods that "sing" to you, and avoid foods that don't. Although not usually written about in conventional nutrition journals or discussed at nutrition conferences, if you observe your body closely, you will notice that some foods feel good to you, even when you're just thinking about them, while others may feel draining.

You may also notice that some foods that normally taste bad will taste better when you are acutely ill. For instance, lemons tend to taste less sour and may even taste sweet when you have a cold or cough. This is but one more example of how nature provides us with hints on how to heal ourselves. This is why it is beneficial to follow your food and drink instincts during acute stages of illness.

Some food may give you energy, but it's important to be mindful of the quality of energy that the particular food gives you. Sugar tends to provide wiry energy, while complex carbohydrates such as whole grains provide more sustained energy. Avoid foods that feel as though a rock is sitting in your stomach; the energy your body is using to digest them may be greater than the nutrients that the food offers.

By following these ten steps to healthy eating, you may not only become healthier, but you may also appreciate the food you eat to a greater extent. Eating to *live* may finally be more important than living to *eat*.

ೞ ೞ

#7

~~~~~~~~~

IF YOU DON'T USE IT,
YOU LOSE IT

*"The only reason I would take up jogging is
so that I could hear heavy breathing again."*
— Erma Bombeck

Not long ago, a typical person might have
felt the urge to rest after a hard day's
work. In today's sedentary times, after a long
day at the office, a person is more apt to feel a
strong desire to exercise.

Exercise alone is considered an essential
ingredient for maintaining and enhancing a
person's overall state of health. It is certainly a
way to improve cardiovascular health, main-

tain overall muscle tone, and aid in weight control. (Exercise alone, however, is not adequate to maintain health, as has been evidenced by the early deaths of many professional and Olympic athletes.)

Exercise plays an even larger role in health than cardiovascular health, muscle tone, and weight control. Most people don't know, for instance, that before the discovery of insulin, physical activity was the primary therapy for diabetes mellitus. Although exercise will not cure diabetes, research has shown that it allows the diabetic to reduce insulin dosages.

Exercise is a treatment recommended by a growing number of psychiatrists and psychologists for depression, so it's kind of funny to think that some people don't want to risk exercising without first obtaining a doctor's approval. With the "side effects" of exercise being a healthier heart, firmer muscles, slimmer figure, and a more positive disposition, more therapists should become coaches . . . and vice versa.

We also know that exercise is important for losing weight. It's been proven that if a person maintains the same calorie intake for one year and simply increases his or her activity level by walking one mile per day, that person would lose approximately ten pounds of fat tissue.

In addition to the various health benefits from exercise, many people engage in physical activity simply because it feels good. Some even report that they get "high" when they exercise. Evidence has shown that physical activity releases endorphins, which are the body's natural painkillers. These opiate-like chemicals actually create a sense of being high; research suggests that some people even become addicted to this feeling. I'm not suggesting that you go that far; the point is that exercise can make you feel great at the same time that it's doing wonderful things for your body.

The greatest obstacle that keeps most people from regular exercise is discipline. Perhaps the thinking is that discipline equates to denial. It doesn't have to be. Put most succinctly, the best way to discipline is to simply remember what you want, what you *really* want. If, for instance, you really want to lose 15 pounds, by focusing on this goal and by reminding yourself of the pleasure that you will feel as a result of losing this weight, one is less distracted by obstacles, and the goal becomes more attainable. (Remember that Weight Watchers motto: *Nothing tastes as good as "thin" feels.)*

One sound piece of advice about exercise is to try to perform an activity once a day to raise your heart rate for at least 15 minutes. (Making love should be considered an activity that is done in *addition* to this minimum daily dose. Fortunately for some people, "if you don't use it you lose it" doesn't apply to such indoor sports.) Choose exercises that you really enjoy, otherwise you won't stick with them. Jogging, swimming, weight-lifting, aerobics, and certain competitive sports build muscular strength and cardiovascular health; while other exercises such as yoga, dance, and various martial arts help to build balance, flexibility, and coordination of mind and body. Make exercise a part of your everyday life, and do those little things to encourage it: Take stairs instead of an elevator, ride your bike for simple chores instead of driving a car, and use a manual lawnmower.

This bit of health wisdom about once-a-day activity applies to mental exercise as much as it does to the physical kind. Just as you may go to a gym or play in a field to exercise, you can also perform mental workouts to improve your memory, comprehension, concentration, and creativity. You can, for instance, make a greater effort to remember people's names and their phone numbers. You can read a newspaper and then several hours later describe to a friend the stories you read, with your own commentary on them. Your concentration can be heightened by meditating for 20 minutes and doing your best to avoid thinking of anything else. You can exercise your own creativity by composing a poem, cooking an exotic dish without a recipe, or rearranging the furniture in your home.

If you don't exercise your mind and stretch and challenge it with short- and long-term efforts, it will become lazy and limp. You can develop "mental sclerosis," just as one can develop arteriosclerosis. Some people who suffer from couch potato-itis may actually seem very intelligent. They are often excellent Trivial Pursuit players (thanks to *Jeopardy*), and they may be great at filling in the Jumble puzzles (thanks to *Wheel of Fortune*). But don't be fooled—they may be TV-smart but intellect-foolish.

So, remember to exercise your body *and* your mind. Considering all the value received from exercising, it is surprising that it isn't taxed!

#8

~~~~~~~

NATURE'S MEDICINE CHEST IS WAITING TO BE OPENED

"Supermarkets are all right, but it's much more fun to shop for food in nature."
— Euell Gibbons

Ralph Waldo Emerson once said, "A weed is an herb whose virtue has not yet been recognized."

As any gardener knows, weeds can be hardy plants that are not easily eliminated from a garden. Perhaps it is this very persistence that constitutes their virtues as well. A weed's ability to grow and even flourish in the smallest crack in the cement is evidence of a certain strength and flexibility. One may wonder if these traits, given the choice of the right weed at the right time, can be transferred to a sick person who ingests it. Perhaps those weeds at our feet are healing us more than we are "heeling" them.

Every culture throughout time has used and even relied upon herbal preparations. In teas, in poultices, in foods, or simply in their raw state, herbs have been found to cure and prevent disease. Like every healing system, however, one has to learn how to use them properly, for some herbs are harmful if overused, and others are poisonous even if ingested in relatively small amounts.

Herbs are finally beginning to be used by a growing number of physicians. Since many conventional drugs are actually derived from herbs, it makes sense to cut out the middleman—the pharmaceutical companies—and go directly to the source. Not only is this cheaper, it's safer.

Whereas drug companies only tend to utilize the most powerful ingredient of an herb, there are often other important and helpful components that are not included in a drug, which often help the body metabolize the primary ingredient and even protect people from poisoning themselves. The herb foxglove (*Digitalis purpurea*), for instance, contains a heart stimulant, digitoxin, which is used in the drug of this name, but it also contains a heart depressant, digitonin. Perhaps this is nature's balancing act and is its way of making it more difficult for humans and other animals to poison themselves. Interestingly, another ingredient in foxglove that is not in the conventional drug is a compound that causes nausea and vomiting. These symptoms warn unsuspecting users that they are taking too much of the herb, thus helping to protect them from taking more of it, which may adversely affect the heart.

If drug companies could patent herbs, they would certainly sponsor more research to discover their value. Many herbs have already been found to have strong antibacterial and antiviral properties. Others have been found to have anti-tumor action, and still others have been shown to reduce cholesterol and blood pressure. In comparison with funds available for research on conventional drugs, herbs do not presently have significant governmental or

corporate support to sponsor research or public education efforts. As a result, except for a
handful of the most well-known herbs, the
public and the medical community remain
ignorant of the value of the hundreds, even
thousands, that are in use today.

Despite the growing interest in herbs, one
can only wonder if there will be opponents to
herbal use. Perhaps one day there will be Dan
D. Lyon, founder of the Herbal Anti-
Defamation League and author of *The Herbifest
Destiny*, who will assert, "Herbs deserve their
place in the sun. They too are God's children.
They should not be separated from their Mother
Earth or enslaved through cultivation. It is also
time that we stop experimentation on herbs.
Such experimentation hurts or kills defenseless
plants." Co-founders Terry Gon, Gary Lick,
Marge Joram, and Val Arian concur, and warn
herb users that their organization is growing
over-ground and underground. Their press
release recently proclaimed, "Our sage advice is
that thyme should be honored, and herbs should
be used gingerly."

Although herbal usage may not be formal-
ly recognized by the medical establishment or

may be criticized by some fringe groups, it is a good idea to cultivate a positive relationship with herbs, for an herb is truly a terrible thing to waste.

#9

~~~~~~~~

THE HAIR OF THE DOG THAT
BITES YOU HEALS YOU

*"To like things like, whatever one may ail,
there is certain help."*
— from *Faust,* by Johann Wolfgang von Goethe

This folk saying about the hair of the dog is an ancient bit of wisdom and an integral part of modern medicine as well.

According to Greek mythology, the Oracle at Delphi proclaimed to Apollo, "That which makes sick shall heal." When the Greek hero Achilles was speared in the ankle, he needed to apply the original spear to his ankle to heal himself. The Mayans, Chinese, and numerous other ancient peoples also commonly treated "like with like." Administering to wasp bites with crushed nests of wasps, and healing jaundice with yellow herbs such as celendine are but a few examples of this ancient principle of pharmacology.

Even a famous story from the Bible highlights this tenet of healing. When Moses came down from Mt. Sinai and saw the Israelites worshiping the golden calf, he became enraged and smashed the calf. He ground it up, diluted it in water, and then told the Israelites to drink it. Moses gave them small doses of what was (symbolically) causing their problems in order to heal them.

The use of "like" to treat "like" is also an integral part of conventional medicine today, as witnessed in the use of immunizations and allergy treatments. Immunizations usually consist of small doses of bacteria or viruses that cause an infection in order to stimulate an immune response that will prevent this infection. Likewise, allergy treatments use minute doses of an allergen to strengthen the adaptive capacities of the body so that it does not react to the substance in a hypersensitive fashion.

Despite these rare uses of the "principle of similars" in conventional medicine, physicians more commonly use drugs that have an opposite action on the person's symptoms. For instance, a person with constipation will be given a laxative, and a person with diarrhea is given something that constipates him. A person with an underactive thyroid gland will be given a thyroid hormone, and a person with an overactive thyroid gland will be given a drug to inhibit excess excretion of a hormone.

The inherent assumption behind the use of opposites in treating sick people is that their body is doing something wrong or that it doesn't know what it is doing. In contrast, the use of similars in treating sick people recognizes that there's an inherent wisdom of the body and a defensive value of its symptoms. Instead of inhibiting this response, using medicines that augment the body's inherent healing capacities promotes real healing, not simply symptom suppression.

Homeopathic medicine is a natural pharmacological science that is entirely based on the principle of similars. It uses small doses of substances that have the capacity, when given in overdose, to cause a pattern of symptoms similar to what the sick person is experiencing. The homeopathic physician's application of the similars concept is, however, distinct from the conventional physician's application of it. Homeopaths use considerably smaller doses of these potentially poisonous substances, and they individualize the prescription to a much more significant degree, taking into account the entire range of the patient's symptoms— not simply devising a generic prescription for a generic disease.

Indeed, one of the challenges of using homeopathic medicines is figuring out the appropriate remedies for each individual. Because the most effective way to apply them is to tailor the prescription according to a sick person's unique pattern of symptoms, there is rarely one medicine for everybody's problem. One person's form of arthritis, headache, or allergy is often distinct from someone else's similar problem and requires a different remedy that addresses this distinction.

In addition to pinpointing the chief complaint of a sick person, the homeopath inquires into the subtle and not-so-subtle other symptoms that the individual is experiencing. For instance, a person with arthritis may experience much swelling in the joints, along with burning and stinging pains, which is worsened by heat and improved by cold application. The person may be awkward, clumsy, and have a tendency to drop things. They may have little or no thirst and be sensitive to touch. This pattern of symptoms is both created by the bee venom (*Apis*) in healthy people and can be healed with homeopathic doses of it.

Using a substance that actually causes arthritis symptoms to treat them may sound strange to some people. However, because symptoms of illness are adaptive responses of the organism to stress or infection, the use of a substance similar to what causes the problem makes sense because this treatment helps to augment the body's natural defensive efforts. Rather than using drugs to suppress symptoms, the law of similars aids in the body's effort to heal itself.

There are numerous homeopathic books, and even some sophisticated computer software, available for guidance in the individualization of a homeopathic medicine for sick people.

Keep in mind that there are right and wrong ways to make use of the similars phenomenon. Do not attempt to treat a pounding headache with a hammer, or mend a broken leg by breaking the other leg. And do not treat a barking cough with the hair of your pet dog. The principle of similars can be a powerful healing tool, but like any tool, you must know how to use it.

Whether or not you utilize the principle of similars phenomenon in healing, it is hoped that you will make use of it when you drive: Remember, always steer *into* a skid, not *away* from it.

#10

~~~~~~

A Little Dab Will Do Ya

"Little by little does the trick."
— Aesop

According to the military version of *Humpty-Dumpty,* after Humpty fell, the General asserted, "All my King's horses and all my King's men cannot put Humpty-Dumpty together again. So, I'm going to need more horses and more men."

Conventional medical solutions tend to be like military solutions. Too often, physicians assert that stronger medicine or more sophisticated medical technology is the answer to a sick person's problem. Sometimes, the best solution is to cease all treatments and let the individual's personal doctor—his or her own body—do its own work.

The human organism already inherently knows how to heal itself; oftentimes it doesn't need the big guns of medicine, but can adequately and effectively heal itself with less biologically disruptive strategies.

Rather than overwhelm the body with powerful drugs or with megadoses of vitamins, it is sometimes more effective to just gently nudge the healing process along. A small dose of the proper nutrient, a stimulus to the appropriate acupuncture point, a catalyst from a well-chosen herb, or an individualized application of a small dose of a homeopathic medicine may be all that is necessary to initiate the healing process.

When small changes occur in certain key biological systems, they create a significant cascade effect on other systems, ultimately leading to major changes. There are, for instance, numerous substances that can, in small doses, stimulate the production of certain enzymes, which will then stimulate liver, kidney, or heart function, which in turn affect in subtle and overt ways every system and cell of the body.

It is interesting to note that submarines communicate with their base and with other submarines using very low radio frequencies because high-frequency radio waves do not penetrate water. And because the human body is 75 to 80 percent water, it might be more effective to use small doses of the right medicine rather than large doses of broad-spectrum drugs.

Homeopathic medicine is a classic example of a medical therapy that utilizes exceedingly small doses of substances, which, when individually prescribed to a person's unique pattern of symptoms, have the capacity to stimulate deep healing. It's not that small doses of any substance will work; it's that small doses of a *key* individualized substance can catalyze a significant reaction.

Another example is the treatment of light on the body. It is widely known in science and medicine that the amount and types of light we absorb affect our brain chemistry and hormonal patterns. Even psychiatrists acknowledge the existence of "winter depression," influenced by lack of sunlight and treated with doses of light. Since sometimes less is more, treatment does not consist of 100 spotlights aimed at the sick person; rather, a couple of low-strength (usually 40 watt), full-spectrum fluorescent tubes for an hour or two a day are all that is usually necessary.

The application of small doses of a specific therapy does not necessarily preclude the value of large doses. The appropriate use of conventional doses of drugs and megadoses of vitamins and minerals have their own place in health care, particularly in treating certain infections or in advanced pathology. However, large doses, especially of certain drugs, are potentially very dangerous.

What is most problematic about large doses of medicine is their tendency to create new symptoms. Although there is a tendency to call these symptoms "side effects," this is actually a misnomer. We arbitrarily differentiate those effects of a drug that we like from those that we don't, and we then call new symptoms "side effects." More precisely, these new symptoms are the result of the drug suppressing the person's present symptoms, or are simply the body's reaction to the drug's toxic ingredients.

Small doses, on the other hand, do not generally carry these dangers, which is a safety factor that should more seriously considered by physicians today, especially since they all promise to "do no harm" as a part of their Hippocratic tradition in medicine.

Ultimately, inherent in strategies that recognize the value and the power of small doses is a healthy respect for the human organism. Using small doses of treatment gently nudges the body in the direction that it knows it must go.

The body knows how to heal itself. It has been doing it for a long, long time. Our job is not to try to take over its job, but to gently encourage the body to do what it already knows.

Indeed, a little dab will do ya!

#11

SOME OF MY BEST
FRIENDS ARE GERMS

*"Each new antibiotic brings into being
literally millions of microscopic
Benedict Arnolds."*
— from *When Antibiotics Fail,* by Marc Lappe, Ph.D.

Like a Hollywood movie that has good guys
and bad guys, the human body plays out
its daily soap opera in which the supporting
role of the "good" bacteria regularly fights the
opportunistic actions of the "bad" bacteria.
The good bacteria actually play an instrumen-
tal part in aiding our digestion of food. They
appear on the skin and oral cavity, helping to

fight infection by creating their own natural antibiotics, and they have been found to stimulate the immune system, serving as a low-level "tonic." The bad bacteria, on the other hand, grow wherever and whenever conditions are favorable for them and cause inflammation, pain, and sometimes death.

There are anywhere from a hundred thousand to one million microscopic organisms on each square centimeter of your skin. There is actually ten times this amount on the parts of the skin that are moist for prolonged periods of time. The webs of the toes, for instance, often carry tens of millions of bacteria of diverse kinds. In total, there are approximately one trillion bacteria on our skin alone, and there are perhaps one hundred trillion more inside the body. Although some people may be horrified to hear that we are literally surrounded by bacteria inside and out, it is important to remember that many of these bacteria not only provide the essential benefits to the body mentioned earlier, but they also help produce vitamin K, biotin, riboflavin, pyridoxine, and other vitamins essential for bodily function.

It seems that bacteria do not have good

public relations agents because they are given a bum rap. They are blamed for a lot of our health problems, yet all of their great deeds often go unnoticed and underappreciated. We actually wouldn't be here without them.

Of course, certain types of bacteria can lead to illness in certain people. Streptococcus can invade the throat, pneumococcus can infiltration lung tissue, and gonococcus can infect mucous membranes. People with bacterial infections are commonly prescribed antibiotics such as ampicillin, tetracycline, and amoxicillin. Although these antibiotics can be literally lifesaving by fighting infection, they do not just cause the death of the bad guys, but of the good guys, too. And unlike a Hollywood movie, the good guys do not always win in the end.

Despite the power of antibiotics, bacteria are often strong enough and smart enough to outwit and out-survive them. Once an antibiotic kills bacteria's friend or relative, the bacteria learn to adapt to the antibiotic and develop a resistance to it. It is as though bacteria have their own internet and can inform each other how to adapt to antibiotics. This is why different and stronger antibiotics are often necessary for treating bacterial infections. This is also why Harvard professor and Nobel Prize winner Walter Gilbert has predicted that sometime in the future, 80 to 90 percent of infections will be resistant to all known antibiotics.

The use of antibiotics can also lead to many long-term health problems. Antibiotics not only knock out the good bacteria with the bad, they also create a more favorable environment for various yeast infections—from opportunists such as *Candida albicans* which leads to vaginitis and numerous other health problems, to *Clostridium difficile*, which leads to colitis.

The use of antibiotics can be likened to the farmer who uses insecticides to rid his swamp of mosquitoes. The insecticide kills the mosquitoes, but the swamp is still a swamp, and a breeding ground for a new infestation. Unless the farmer does something to change the nature of the swamp or adds a predator such as frogs to eat mosquito eggs, the farmer will continue to have a problem. A more ecological and holistic solution is necessary for real change to occur.

Likewise, rather than attacking the bacteria with antibiotics, it may be more effective to consider various natural therapies that strengthen the person's immune system and thereby improve the ability of the body to defend itself more effectively. Various herbs, including licorice root and Echinacea; certain foods, such as shiitake mushrooms and garlic; and individualized treatments of homeopathic medicines and acupuncture have all been shown to stimulate immune response. Also, methods that calm, energize, or ultimately balance one's emotional and mental state may be valuable. Even many other modern-day physicians and scientists have suggested that a person's psychological state could influence resistance to microbes. Meditation, relaxation, and other stress management approaches are potentially effective strategies to both prevent and treat certain infectious conditions.

Despite the value of these various alternatives, antibiotics are at times the most effective way to treat certain infections. But just because you are using antibiotics doesn't mean that you should ignore natural therapies. In fact, one way to reduce their possible side effects of antibiotics is to take acidophilus—one of the friendly types of intestinal bacteria—available either in pill form or in yogurt or miso. By replenishing your intestines with these beneficial bacteria, you may not only feel better sooner, you may be less likely to get reinfected.

Making matters a bit more complicated, however, are the actions of a majority of American farmers who feed massive amounts of antibiotics to their chickens, pigs, and cows as a way to prevent infection. When consumers eat the meat, milk, or eggs from these animals, they also ingest trace amounts of antibiotics. Many scientists have suggested that these small amounts enable the harmful bacteria in us to adapt to larger medicinal doses of antibiotics. As a result, conventional doses of antibiotics may not work as well for us, and instead, more powerful doses or stronger antibiotics become increasingly necessary.

There are problems inherent in antibiotic treatment and in any method that ignores the interrelationships of life. Chief Seattle was thought to have said, "We are part of the web of life. We are not the weavers. When a part of the web is destroyed, a part of ourselves is hurt." Whether he was the actual author of this statement or not, these words have real meaning for both our external and internal environments—our bodies.

As much as we may "boo" and "hiss" when the bad bacteria enters the picture, it should not simply be considered the "Big Bad Wolf." This type of bacteria alerts us to a personal weakness that has enabled it to grow. It can challenge and ultimately strengthen our immune system, and encourage a microbial diversity that can actually lead to biological stability.

This information is not meant to imply that antibiotics aren't valuable, lifesaving drugs. However, it is absolutely vital that we use antibiotics judiciously by using alternatives first and by only resorting to these drugs in medical emergencies.

#12

~~~~~

Make Friends with Your Pain

*"Sometimes you pain doesn't make
your life unbearable; your life
makes your pain unbearable."*
— David Bresler, Ph.D.

The word *pain* is derived from the Latin
word *poena*, which means "punishment."
Whether pain should be thought of as a punishment is debatable, but we know that it certainly hurts to have it, and it usually feels like
a punishment, whether the person has done
something to deserve it or not. In ancient
times, people thought that pain was caused by

demons who had possessed them. And if
didn't pay your exorcist to get rid of
demons, you got repossessed!

Pain is nature's way of making you
notice. It is a warning—sometimes a
warning—that something is wrong. It
symptom and a signal, and it demands
attention!

Headaches, backaches, arthritis,
menstrual cramps are the most frequent
syndromes. Most people today treat their
with one or more of the various
inflammatory medicines, a.k.a. painkill
However, because pain itself is only a sy
tom, painkillers may reduce the discomfor
do nothing to heal the source of pain. In
suppressing the symptoms of pain can d
the pain and the disease deeper into the per
The body eventually adapts to the painki
and soon needs stronger and stronger dose
order to achieve a similar degree of relief.
body also becomes addicted to these dr
ultimately causing new types of discom
and dysfunction for which a person all
often takes additional drugs to treat. A
cycle has been created, and it is sometimes

ficult to break.

Denying pain is equally ineffective. Some people ignore their pain. They assume that nothing is wrong, that there is nothing that they should change about themselves, and that the pain they are having is only a temporary glitch that will soon disappear. Famed psychiatrist Carl Jung once said, "If you don't come to terms with your shadow, it will appear in your life as your fate." Until a person sheds light on the shadow of pain, its fateful return will be a continual reminder of something amiss. It has been said, "Denial ain't just a river in Egypt." It runs deep and wide, and you cannot wash away your pain by denial. Unless and until awareness replaces denial, the pain will demand attention one way or another.

The challenge of pain is to try to comprehend what it is saying. What is not in balance in your life? Is there something that you need to change within yourself, or is there something outside you that either needs to be avoided or changed? Does the specific location and kind of pain have any special meaning to you? And why did the pain start now?

Seeking to understand pain can itself be

therapeutic. It can turn a difficult situation into a learning and growing experience. It is, of course, difficult to understand one's pain, but it is a real problem when people do not even try. Perhaps this is why Bill Wilson, co-founder of Alcoholics Anonymous, once said, "Years ago I used to commiserate with all people who suffered. Now I commiserate only with those who suffer in ignorance, who do not understand the purpose and ultimate utility of pain."

Whatever the source or meaning of pain, it represents a certain wisdom of the body and mind to defend itself and to adapt to stress or infection. Whatever the nature of the pain, it is decidedly more effective to appreciate it rather than resist it. Resistance creates additional tension and usually additional pain. Loving attention, on the other hand, can have a noticeably soothing and healing effect.

Loving one's pain is certainly easier to say than do. It seems a lot simpler to feel irritated and angry about the pain, depressed and despairing about how horrible it is, and fearful and anxious about how long it will persist. But just as easily as a person in pain can assume that life is a series of problems, this person can also be intrigued by the challenge of life as a series of adventures. Instead of fretting about the pain, the person can be curiously seeking out ways to deal with it.

There is also something wonderfully healing about simply giving "positive vibrations" to pain. Although this may sound hokey, a person in pain is usually willing to do some odd things in an effort to obtain relief. Since resisting or fighting pain is like pulling at a knot from both ends, learning to love the knot sometimes loosens its grip.

As heroes in many a fairy tale have reflected, "You don't have to hate the dragon to love the princess." Likewise, you don't have to hate the pain to love the challenge it creates. This may be an important first step in learning to deal with pain most effectively.

#13

~~~~~~~~~

TAKE LAUGHTER SERIOUSLY

*"You don't stop laughing because
you grow old; you grow old because
you stop laughing."*
— Michael Prichard

When faced with adversity, members of most species choose fight or flight. Humans, however, have a third choice: laughter. A good belly laugh reduces tension. Finding humor in a stressful situation often diffuses it.

Many people don't take laughter seriously. They usually think that it's kid stuff or unprofessional or simply inappropriate, considering all of the world's problems. Yet, humor is an integral part of our humanness; it can give us a uniquely healthy perspective on a real problem. It may "break the ice" and create a more trusting relationship. It may also create a sense of joy so that even if one is defeated or in pain, joy and its memories will provide an important salve.

It is not simply a coincidence that laughter is thought to "break you up." Laughter stimulates a healthy internal jogging. As with other forms of jogging, laughter leads temporarily to faster and deeper breathing and greater oxygen supply throughout the bloodstream. Vigorous and frequent laughter can even help to burn up as many calories as many common physical activities. Studies have even shown that simple smiling creates beneficial changes in body chemistry, even when the smile is faked. That curved line of a smile sometimes straightens everything out.

Humor and laughter are especially important when a person is ill. Funny movies and the laughter that they create have been shown to improve immune function and increase a person's ability to withstand pain. The only side effects that this treatment is known to have are joyful memories. Although you might say, "It hurts when I laugh," more often people hurt when they don't.

Unfortunately, it seems that the majority of physicians and scientists are more interested in studying the negative emotional states that may lead to disease rather than studying those positive emotional states that may lead to healthier and happier people. But even the Bible acknowledges that "a merry heart doeth good like a medicine" (Proverbs 17:22). Perhaps doctors in the future will be as likely to prescribe Robin Williams, Woody Allen, or Marx Brothers movies as they are to prescribe drugs.

Laughter is just as infective as germs and can be wonderfully contagious. It will rarely cure you on its own, but it sure will make your problems more bearable. As the saying goes, angels can fly because they take themselves lightly.

Laughter is not just an external or temporary Band-Aid; it is effective long-term medicine. Studies have shown that people who are hopeful and optimistic tend to live longer and healthier lives. Perhaps the saying should be changed to "he who laughs, lasts."

Not only does laughter *feel* good, it is *good* for you. Have you had your minimum daily dose today?

#14

~~~~~~~~~~

RELAX, BUT DON'T
TURN INTO MUSH

*"Stress is the spice of life.
Complete freedom from stress is death."*
— Hans Selye, M.D.

Everybody is always telling us to relax. If
you're depressed about something that just
happened, relax. If you're worried about something that may occur in the future, relax. Even
if you're extremely excited about something,
someone is bound to tell you to cool down
and relax.

Sounds great, but the goal of life is more
than feeling relaxed. And what's worse, if you

relax too much, you may turn into mush.

Stress has become the "bad guy." We are supposed to avoid it, reduce it, and manage it. It seems that stress has been blamed for just about everything. Actually, stress is an integral part of life and living. It is stress that encourages us to go beyond our perceived limits; it challenges us.

The Chinese character for "crisis" is actually a combination of two words: *danger* and *opportunity*. Stress also is a sign of danger and an opportunity to grow. Although stress can lead to discomfort and disease, it can also be seen as a challenge that can make you stronger.

Stress only becomes a problem when you can't make good use of it. Just as the body gets fatigued from overwork, so does the brain. The brain can burn as many calories during intense concentration or great anxiety as do muscles during exercise. Perhaps weight-loss farms of the future will have chess games for those who wish to concentrate, and even surrogate mothers-in-law for those who want to experience the aerobic effects of anxiety. The dark side of concentration and anxiety, however, is that thinking too much can exhaust a person, and too-frequent emotions can be draining.

Here's where relaxation can be helpful. Sitting or lying comfortably, closing your eyes, breathing deeply and slowly, and being in a quiet environment are important and helpful in achieving some degree of relaxation. The initial stages of relaxation enable you to slow down and literally catch your breath.

However, frequent or distressing thoughts all too often rush to the forefront of one's mind. There are various strategies for dealing with this mental chatter, and some people devote their lives to perfecting their ability to create an inner calm. Some focus on their breathing, others on a specific mantra (a phrase that is continually repeated), and still others on a pleasurable feeling or experience they've had.

Another strategy for dealing with incessant mental chatter is to try to let go of any and all thoughts as they arise. Although they will inevitably come back, it is best to let them go again, to avoid trying to problem-solve during this time, and to simply *be*, without trying to think, feel, or do anything. Interestingly, thinking, feeling, and doing nothing is much harder than one would . . . think.

Although you might certainly wonder how and why doing nothing can be of any benefit, a growing body of scientific evidence has begun to confirm the therapeutic value of deep relaxation. Besides lowering blood pressure, it can also stimulate the body's own immune system. It is almost as though relaxation helps us get out of the way of the body's inherent self-healing capacities. Just as the body is more able to heal itself during sleep, conscious relaxation provides the body with a great opportunity for healing.

Learning to relax is one important strategy, but like every strategy, it has its limitations. Imagine how awful it would be if dictators learned to relax just so that they could feel more comfortable acting out their oppression. Think how terrible it would be if employers learned to relax and then gave their employees ulcers while avoiding them themselves. Consider how horrible it would be if politicians learned to relax just so they could avoid raising their own blood pressure while they dipped their hands into public funds.

Relaxation is invaluable for getting to that centered place within, to that inner sense of peace and security, but unless one acts from this relaxed point in a purposeful manner, relaxation only becomes an escape—not a way to resolve a bad situation.

So . . . relax, but don't turn into mush.

#15

~~~~~~~~~

It's the Little Things That Get You

*"Rule #1 is, don't sweat the small stuff.
Rule #2 is, it's all small stuff. And if you can't
fight and you can't flee, flow."*
— R. S. Eliot

Dances with wolves are easy; dances with elephants, however, are more difficult. There are only two types of people who dance with elephants: quick people and smashed people. Luckily, most of us don't have to dance with elephants. Although most of us can differentiate big danger from small danger, the little stresses that people experience every day can often sneak up on them and wipe them out just as effectively as the big ones can.

We all know that major stresses in our lives, such as deaths in the family, divorces, or tax audits, can have a significant impact on our health. However, the accumulation of the smaller stresses, especially when prolonged, can have a similar significant and detrimental effect. The stress felt driving in rush-hour traffic, talking to a person who is being difficult, dealing with various family problems, and keeping a home clean and organized every day can add wrinkles to our faces, anxieties to our stomachs, and wobbles to our knees. This extra weight is sometimes enough to topple even those of us who are doing everything we can to maintain life's balancing act.

A tyrannical executive was once asked if he had high blood pressure. He said, "No, but I am a carrier." All too often, employers, friends, or even strangers do certain things that not only stress others, but also aggravate an underlying problem that previously had been lying dormant. A little stress can set off a chain reaction. The mouse is roaring.

Little problems add up to create major

dilemmas unless they are dealt with as they occur. The mind has a natural tendency to try to work out and complete stressful experiences. Leftover, dangling situations obscure our vision of the world and force us to reexperience those past situations until they are made right. Our dreams and nightmares commonly become the theater in which the leftover dramas of our daily life are replayed.

One way to deal with the small day-to-day stresses is, first of all, to know that they are there, even if you cannot initially acknowledge where they are. Once you realize that you are experiencing subtle and sometimes not-so-subtle stresses, you can decide to do something about them. One or more of the following techniques may be helpful after you have acknowledged their potential existence:

1. Head them off at the pass. Prevent the little stresses by anticipating and then avoiding them. Determine what your most common little stresses are, and do whatever is necessary to prevent them or handle them as they develop. If, for instance, you have to drive in rush-hour traffic, listen to a relaxing tape while you drive. If you are dealing with a difficult person, diffuse their negativity by "killing them with kindness" or by injecting a little (or a lot) of humor into the situation.

2. Do a body-check. At least once a day, perform an exercise in which you close your eyes and move your consciousness to various parts of your body, looking for areas that feel stiff or stuck. Shake the area, massage it, breathe into it, and then relax it. Consider how and why a particular part of your body is feeling blocked.

3. Do a life-check. Just as many people have "to do" lists in their daily life, it is helpful to have a life-check list in which you assess how you are doing, what barriers are in the way of where you want to be, and how you plan to get over or around these obstacles.

ඕ ඕ ඕ

We usually focus on the big problems in our lives and try to figure out what to do about them. Too often we neglect how the small things add up to create big problems. Even though an elephant's fear of a mouse may not be well founded, it's important to keep in mind that minor issues can sneak up on you and affect your health more readily than major problems can. Remember: You can sit on a mountain, but you can't sit on a tack.

#16

~~~~~

SELF-MEDICATING
WITH SELF-ESTEEM

*"If you put a small value upon yourself,
rest assured that the world will not
raise the price."*
— Anonymous

How you feel about yourself may actually affect the way your body defends itself against the various stresses and infective organisms that surround it. During infection, the body's white blood cells identify foreign microorganisms and then seek to devour or excrete them. The body's ability to identify its own cells distinct from foreign organisms or substances is vital for the healthy functioning of the organism.

But just as a person may sometimes experience a personal identity crisis, the body at times has difficulty differentiating itself from foreign life forms. Without the body's ability to detect "self" from "non-self," a person is prone to infection and disease. Since the body and mind are inexorably connected, one can only wonder if low self-esteem—a diminished sense of identity—can lead to weaker immune function. As above, so below.

On the other hand, a high level of self-esteem, or a stronger sense of self, can lead to more vigorous immune response. While this doesn't mean that people with high self-esteem will never get sick, it does mean that they will be better equipped to deal with whatever stresses or diseases they encounter.

Each threat to our health can strengthen our ability to survive. Each symptom of disease, though painful and discomforting, is the organism's best efforts to respond to stress or infection. Likewise, each doubt about ourselves can be approached as a challenge to overcome. These symptoms and doubts can constitute an important personal defense and a potentially helpful lesson on how to live in the world.

Developing high self-esteem is particularly difficult if you have been continually told that you are a loser. It is helpful to know, however, that a "winner" in self-esteem is rarely a "born winner," but is often one who is successful because of the blood, sweat, and years that have been applied to a particular goal.

For instance, the first Western man to scale Mt. Everest failed the first two times. After the second time, he addressed his sponsors, the Board of Directors of the National Geographical Society. Rather than berate himself or apologize for his failures, he simply showed them a picture of Mt. Everest and said, "This mountain will never grow another inch, but with each failure, I learn and I grow." On his third attempt, he reached the top.

If you fail at something or if people call you a loser, it's easy to feel terrible about yourself, get depressed, and become ill. The sickness cycle is created when you feel unhappy and insecure and then become more depressed as a result of the illness.

A way out of this cycle will sound trite, but it's true: We need to remind ourselves that we really are all winners. When you think about it, each of our fathers created millions and millions of sperm, each of our mothers created egg after egg after egg . . . and *we* were the ones who made it! Each of us is worthy of a gold medal.

Self-esteem cannot be given to you or be bought, sold, or traded. If it is based solely on material successes, personal appearance, fame, or occupation, these transient and superficial factors provide only a temporary and often false sense of self-value. And if you pretend to have self-esteem, you just fool yourself. Ultimately, your life and your health function as your own lie detector test.

Self-esteem is inevitably an inside job, and this inner feeling radiates outward, creating a healthier body and a state of contagious good vibes. Self-esteem won't raise the dead, but it will raise everything else.

Don't just stand there—full esteem ahead.

෯෯෯

#17

~~~~~~~~

FOLLOW YOUR BLISS

*"Dwell as near as possible to the channel
in which your life flows."*
— Henry David Thoreau

"Be here now" was a personal and spiritual motto for many people in the 1970s, and "Follow your bliss" is taking its place today. In addition to simply appreciating the present, "Follow your bliss," means to discover and act upon that which gives your life meaning. It does not mean simply doing things that give you pleasure; it means following the yearnings of your heart, your mind, and your very soul. Just as food feeds the body, living your passion is food for the soul. Such soul food is *real* health food.

When people have purpose and meaning in their life, it is amazing how much they can and will endure to attain their goal. There are innumerable examples of people overcoming their devastating pain or life-threatening illness in order to finish their important work. This work might be anything from caring for one's children or painting a picture to writing a book or healing others.

Meaning and purpose in your life can be found in your family, job, community, or spiritual path—whatever it is, it directly affects your health. A U.S. government study, for instance, showed that the best indicator of health status did not relate to a person's diet, amount of exercise performed, or stress management efforts, but to the degree of work satisfaction that the individual enjoyed. Although this information may surprise some, it will make complete sense to others. Not only do a considerable number of people spend more time at work than anywhere else, but personal identity, self-worth, and sense of community are an integral part of their profession. A job is not simply what a person does to earn a living, it is also a connection and contribution to the world. To some fortunate people, their job is even an important part of their mission in life.

While some people may relax for 30 minutes a day, the five to ten hours spent at work have a much greater and enduring effect on one's life and health. It's no wonder, then, that it is more healthful to take your job and love it than it is to take it and . . . well, you know. Indeed, finding work that you love can be one of the most powerful healing strategies.

Perhaps it is no accident that the word *vocation* is derived from a Latin word that means "a calling." Whether your calling is your work or not, having a mission or path in life creates the ability to shine light into whatever darkness you may be experiencing. Doing what one loves creates a special happiness and a unique connectedness to others as the result of the heartfelt efforts that are being made.

Following your bliss enables bliss to follow you. Not only do people who have a sense of purpose in life often seem happier within themselves, but they also radiate a contagious aliveness that infects those around them.

Although people who are following their bliss get sick and die just like anyone else, their quality of life is significantly different. Sometimes this improved quality of life improves one's health, but perhaps of greater importance, this enhanced level of wellness helps you to better achieve your life purpose.

Most people hope to attain whatever their life's goal is, although it is not as important to be "successful" as it is to heartily try. Mahatma Gandhi once said, "Everything we do is futile, but we must do it anyway." This is when you know that you are doing your life's work: when you are so involved and so clear and certain about your mission that the process of getting there is, in itself, fulfilling.

Although people commonly have doubts about how much a single person can do, JFK reminded us of the importance of each person's actions when he said, "One person with courage makes a majority." Indeed, each of our actions makes an imprint upon the world.

Having a calling, mission, or goal in life helps give you a purpose. Rather than simply floating aimlessly from one experience to another, a person with direction is going somewhere, and mysteriously enough, a person with direction is often directed. A 16th-century French writer, Michel Montaigne, once wrote, "No wind blows on a ship without a port of destination." It is as though having a calling, a mission, or a life goal somehow helps to create a wind that helps propel you there.

Such is the mystery of life. How now, great Tao.

#18

~~~~~

THE POWER OF PRAYER IS
GREATER THAN YOU THINK

*"Every time I pray to God, I find that
I am talking to myself."*
— Peter O'Toole in *The Ruling Class*

Henry Ford once said, "Those who say they can do something and those who say they can't are both right." The point here is that every thought is a prayer. Every thought creates biochemical processes that subtly and sometimes significantly change the way you are. You do not have to clasp your hands together in order to pray. Simply visualizing or wishing for something can be the first step to making it happen. Prayer, however, is more than just thinking, visualizing, or wishing. It is a profound expression of the soul's desires or needs, and it is a deeply felt expression of gratitude or a call for help.

People commonly pray for health, either for others or for themselves, and research has shown that prayer can have significant healing effects. Whether it's because an outside force helps the person heal or because of the love emanating from oneself or others, prayer can work.

To whom one prays seems to be secondary to the act of praying. For every individual who says that their God is the most effective healer, there are others who say the same thing about *their* God. And for every individual who claims that an external force has healed them, there are others who believe that the healing came from within. One belief system is probably no more correct than the other, for if this force is as all-pervasive, as many people claim, perhaps everyone is talking about the same force, just with different names.

A prayer usually contains a goal, an image, and a profound desire for something to happen. You, however, must be willing to accept whatever happens, and to surrender to the truth and the selflessness of love behind the prayer in order for it to have the best chance to work its wonders. Any anxiety or denial about what is happening may tarnish the clarity of the prayer, and any selfish love may diminish its power.

As we think and wish and pray, we create the initial building blocks that lead to action. A thought or prayer is the Pavlov's bell that gets a person salivating for what he wants. Once this salivation begins, the hunger must lead to action. Just because you're hungry doesn't mean you will always get food, though. A thought or prayer will lie dormant unless you act to create it or put yourself in a position to receive it.

As some people believe, Determination + Prayer + Action = Result. Without the determination and action, prayer alone usually becomes a visualization without the manifestation.

Praying for health requires a certain amount of nonattachment to the goal. A man, for instance, may pray for relief for his headache, but if he is extremely anxious for his prayers to be answered, his anxiety can impede the healing. Likewise, a mother may pray so desperately for the health of her sick child that her fears about what may happen may be felt by the child and interfere with the potential for healing.

The good news (and the bad news) about prayer is that you often get much more than what you pray for. Like the child who prayed for a horse and was disappointed to get the flies that came with it. Or the person who prayed for less severe psoriasis symptoms, only to develop a more painful arthritic condition soon afterwards.

One also must be clear and precise about whatever is being prayed for. For instance, my friend Judith prayed to marry a rich man. Within a year, she married a man named Rich. Another friend prayed for a committed relationship. Shortly thereafter, she adopted a two-year-old child. Remember that saying: Be careful what you ask for because you may get it? Well, it's true!

A certain amount of clarity, precision, persistence, and luck can always improve one's chances for getting prayers answered. However, whether you get the "it" for which you are praying or not, perhaps you already have it, perhaps you don't really need it, or perhaps you will receive greater benefits from *not* having it.

#19

~~~~~~~~

EVERYBODY IS A
GRANDMOTHER

*"He who neglects to drink of the spring
of experience is likely to die of thirst in
the desert of ignorance."*
— Ling Po

Everybody is a grandmother because
everyone has their own sage advice and
personal experience. Will Rogers once said,
"Everybody is ignorant, just on different subjects." But the opposite of this statement is
also true: Everybody is an expert, just on different subjects.

We all have our own experience with

respect to healing techniques that work and those which don't. For example, simply living 40 years means that a person has experienced 40 cold and flu seasons, 80 allergy seasons (that's spring and fall), and innumerable stomachaches, headaches, coughs, and injuries.

We too often give more credence to professionals with a degree than to people with experience. This logic was classically demonstrated when the wizard in *The Wizard of Oz* gave the Scarecrow a diploma instead of a brain. We too often assume that a diploma means brains. But the best knowledge comes from experience. It has been said: "Tell me, and I will forget. Show me, and I will try to understand. Involve me, and I will learn." Experience gives us all the opportunity of involvement, and it gives us a chance to receive real knowledge. Ultimately, though, experience is not what happens to a person; it is what you *do* with what happens to you.

One problem with using experience as a guide is that the final exam often comes first and is then followed by the lesson. Ralph Waldo Emerson seemed to understand this paradox when he said, "Life is a succession of lessons which must be lived to be understood."

If you do not have the experience yourself, seek others who may have it. Such people are often older than you are, but not always. It is usually preferred to heed the advice of those who have come out the other side of the experience rather than those who are experts in living with the problem, although any experience carries its own wisdom on how to do something . . . or how not to do it.

Knowledge and wisdom do not simply come from positive experiences. As former U.S. Senator Bob Packwood once appropriately said prior to leaving office, "Judgment comes from experience, and great judgment comes from bad experience."

Learning from another's experience can be helpful but can also have its risks. Because each human and each situation is so unique, what may work for another may be ineffective or even dangerous to you. Here's where common sense, intuition, and your own personal experiences are vital in choosing strategies to heal yourself.

Learning from a book, even this book (!), has its limitations. The concepts about healing and the strategies to effect it that are described here may not work for you. This will not mean that you are abnormal or incurable (or that this is not a good book); it may simply mean that you should seek out people with other sets of experience. Talk to your grandmother or someone else's grandmother.

Everybody, indeed, has his or her own experience. Everybody is a grandmother with her or his own recipe for health and good living. This isn't to say that every recipe will work for you or that it always worked for your grandmother. But if you think about it, your grandmother made it to her ripe old age by doing *something* right. When everything else fails, consider emulating success.

#20

~~~~~~

OBSESSION WITH HEALTH CAN BE SICKENING

"A halo only has to fall a couple of inches to become a noose."
— Farmer's Almanac

If there was an organization called Healthaholics Anonymous, it would, no doubt, be immensely popular. A growing number of people are becoming more than concerned about their health; they are becoming obsessed with it. These people are not just interested in exploring specific health strategies; they are "into" them. They are "into" macrobiotics, "into" massage, or "into" yoga.

Such people can become macroneurotic or needy kneaders; being "into" yogic postures can create special problems because it may be difficult to get out of them.

There is a real difference between concern about health and obsession with it. Some people obsessed about nutrition believe that there are only two types of food: those that are good for you and those that cause a slow, painful death. Some people obsessed with stress management strategies spend so much energy managing their life that they neglect to live it. Some people obsessed with vitamins turn useful supplements into potentially dangerous substances. And some people obsessed with meditating end up sitting on all their other needs.

The most common obsession in the health area has to do with food. Anyone who starts to research the various theories about nutrition ultimately discovers that almost any food is thought to be poison, according to one school of thought or another. Meat is poison to vegetarians; milk products are poisons to vegans; tomatoes and eggplant are poisons to macrobiotics; cooked foods are poisons to the raw foodists; and on and on.

Anyone can think of one reason or another that any food may not be good for you, but one can also consider ways that most foods provide certain benefits. Meats may have too much fat, but they are also an excellent source of iron. Eggs may have cholesterol in them, but they have lecithin in them that helps digest cholesterol and other fats more effectively. Cooked foods may lose certain nutrients, but they make other nutrients assimilate better. Ice cream may have a lot of fat, but it can be an important "mental health food."

Perhaps most dangerous for people obsessed with nutrition is the amount of fear they ingest with their meals. Fears of pesticides, hormones, fluoridation, chlorination, radiation, and heavy metals are ingested with every meal. One can only wonder if their emotional state is poisoning them more than the foods and drinks they ingest.

Obsession with exercise is also commonly experienced. Although this obsession may seem more beneficial than harmful, the dark side of exercise fanaticism becomes evident when physical activity begins to dominate a person's life. When you begin to live for the gym or your 50 miles a week, when your personal relationships begin to suffer because your exercise routine always comes first, when you exercise in spite of injury or start climbing the walls when you can't work out, you may wake up one morning to discover that the only thing left in your life *is* exercise. And this is seriously unhealthy. The purpose of good health and exercise is to *enrich* your life, not for exercise to *become* your life.

The exercise addiction is particularly problematic when you become obsessed solely with workouts and neglect other valuable ways to build and maintain health. The athlete who eats junk food and the bodybuilder who can't relax are two classic examples of this obsession. Although there are certainly worse addictions than exercise, any action that limits a person's freedom diminishes health.

One way to detect if you are obsessed with health is if you are passionate about a single health discipline—be it nutrition, exercise, homeopathy, herbs, yoga, or whatever—but ignore other health strategies. Health is feeling whole; it is a balance of the physical, emotional, mental, and spiritual aspects of our being.

It is certainly healthy to be concerned about your health, but obsessions and addictions fragment the wholeness of health and ultimately disrupt the quality of your life. As members of Healthaholics Anonymous might someday say, "May God grant me the serenity to accept the health conditions I cannot change, the courage to heal myself of the ones I can, and the wisdom to know the difference."

#21

~~~~~~~~

A POLLUTED PLANET CREATES POLLUTED PEOPLE

"The creature that wins against its environment destroys itself."
— Gregory Bateson

Our planet is not called "Mother Earth" for symbolic reasons only. We have been born to and from this Earth. We are not simply *on* this planet but *of* this planet. Unless we learn to take care of our home, we will all be prematurely buried six feet deep underneath it.

Just as the human body can become ill, so can a planet's body. Global pollution is turning the Earth prematurely gray. Our planet is presently experiencing a global warming, a fever and inflammatory condition that is slowly cooking us all. The life-giving blood of the planet is in great disorder as a result of water pollution, and the planet's respiration is being choked by air pollution. Our planet's most efficient oxygen-manufacturing plants are the rain forests, and they are being wiped out at an alarming rate. Also, anemic soil conditions are creating biological malnourishment and chronic fatigue, turning lush plant life into deserts. Overpopulation is creating congestion, a type of constipation in which increased waste buildup leads to diminished capabilities of elimination. Toxic waste sites have become the planet's newest infections, resulting in corrosive materials opportunistically oozing and seeping out wherever they can.

Of greatest long-term potential danger to our Mother Earth is nuclear waste storage, which creates a hereditary disturbance that can strike at the heart of the planet's life. Such storage becomes the Earth's legacy. It is a Pandora's Box that must never be opened, and yet, we can only hope that time and circumstance does not disturb or open it.

Like the human body's response to symptoms, the planet's symptoms are its efforts to call attention to a problem, to reduce it, and to attempt to heal itself. Sometimes, however, the stress is persistent, and the Earth cannot heal itself adequately or rapidly enough against the ravages of our progressive human race. It adapts, it deforms itself, and it rids itself of any vulnerable life form—even if it means destroying its children to save itself.

Efforts to control, outwit, or dominate nature are ultimately detrimental to human health and survival. Human health is more dependent on the health of the planet than vice versa. Until and unless we learn to live in harmony with our home planet, we will be expelled from this once pristine Garden of Eden.

We are finally waking up to the need for a healthy home, both for our own and our planet's benefit. It is now becoming patriotic to conserve energy, to recycle, and to use biodegradable products.

There are innumerable decisions that each person makes every day that can slightly and sometimes greatly reduce Earth's resources. We must make these decisions more consciously so that we learn to live in greater harmony with our home.

One important and relatively simple way to help Earth heal (and yourself, too) is to eat less meat or omit it from your diet entirely. Eating lower on the food chain is less energy intensive, less polluting, and more ecologically beneficial than our standard American diet. Not only must more people purchase recyclable products more often, we must also consume less. Not only must more people conserve energy, we must seek alternative forms, such as solar and wind energy. There are numerous books now available that provide more suggestions for how you can help heal Earth in your daily life.

Acting as individuals, we must also try to reduce the toil and trouble that our lifestyle creates for our environment. We must also encourage the companies for which we work and other companies with whom we do business to become ecologically concerned, both in the products they create and how they manufacture them. Ultimately, every action and every purchase must be considered for their environmental effect.

Although these efforts are vital for our survival and for that of our children, we must do more. Due to the already present environmental problems, we must now go on a planetary diet. We must extend our efforts beyond simply maintaining Earth as it is to ways that will help her recover from her severe illness. It is incumbent upon us all to strongly encourage governments to make more forthright efforts to clean up the mess we have created.

It has been said that one person's right to wave a fist ends where another's nose begins. Because everything in this home planet is so interconnected, our nose, metaphorically speaking, is actually much more vulnerable than most of us realize—not just to fists, but to various environmental assaults. Unless we learn to live lightly on our planet, our children will carry the heavy burden of our conscious and unconscious indiscretions.

#22

~~~~~~~~~~

LOVE IS NATURE'S PSYCHOTHERAPY

"Love cures people—both the one who gives it and the one who receives it."
— Karl Menninger, M.D.

Love begets love, hate begets hate, and beget begets beget.

Everything is contagious—not just germs, but good vibes and bad vibes, too. Simply witness what happens when a person begins laughing hysterically, and watch how this action gets others to laugh or at least smile. Also witness what happens when someone is expressing hatred for another, and notice how those in the vicinity tighten their bodies, develop a defensive posture, and maybe clutch another's hand.

Loving and hating are not just emotional states—both have direct physical effects on the body. Just as fear creates the fight-or-flight reaction, feelings of hate create an armoring of the body that tenses the musculature, raises blood pressure, shortens and speeds respiration, and creates a clear psychological distance between people. Feelings of love, in contrast, reduce tension, decrease blood pressure, lengthen and slow breathing, and blur the distinction between one person and another. Not only does hate hurt others, it hurts the person feeling it, while love benefits both the giver and receiver.

Although most people do not know how to tell their body to heal itself, they do know how to love, and this can set of wheels of healing in motion. As Yale surgeon Bernie Siegel likes to remind people, "If I told patients to raise their blood levels of immune globulins or killer T-cells, no one would know how. But if I can teach them to love themselves and others fully, the same changes happen automatically. The truth is: Love heals."

Love can heal physical, emotional, and spiritual pain. Love of self and love from or for others can soothe physical pain, enrich emotional life, and help connect one person with another. Although love has powerful side effects, they are all *positive* side effects. And when love doesn't heal completely, at least it makes the pain a lot easier to handle.

Learning to love is, however, a lot more difficult than it seems, especially for people who haven't received much love themselves. It is also problematic for those who have received what was called love, but it tended to smother more than soothe them. Perhaps the best place to start is by learning to love yourself. By being loving, a person makes him or herself more lovable. Through giving, a person receives. By being joyful, a person shares joy with others. It seems so obvious, yet it is so elusive to too many people.

"As you sow, so shall you reap" is an old saying that reminds us that what is put into something is what is received from it. The hands that give away flowers retain the fragrance of the gift.

Bad vibes can be just as contagious as

good ones. The worst thing that an S.O.B. can do is turn *you* into an S.O.B. Anger, fear, and hate are all contagious, too, although each of us can learn to be more resistant to these "infections." By expressing compassion, anger is dissipated. By seeking to understand the unknown, fear disappears. By loving, hate evaporates.

The price one pays for hating others is loving oneself less. Even worse, the body feels this emotion and expresses it as pain and disease.

Perhaps one day soon, more doctors will prescribe love for their patients. It may not cure them all, but it is a good place to start.

RECOMMENDED READING

I hope that this book has inspired you to learn more about natural healing. Some of the following books provide an overview of natural healing concepts, while others recommend specific strategies for healing. This list is not meant to be complete; it consists of those books that I have personally read, appreciated, and used.

GENERAL HEALTH

Achterberg, Jeanne. *Imagery in Healing*. Boston: Shambhala, 1985.

Becker, Robert O. *Cross Currents: The Perils of Electropollution, The Promise of Electromedicine.* New York: Jeremy Tarcher, 1990.

Brown, Chip. *Afterwards, You're a Genius*, New York: Riverhead, 1998.

Castleman, Michael. *Cold Cures*. New York: Fawcett, 1987.

Castleman, Michael. *Nature Cures*. Emmaus, PA: Rodale, 1996.

Dadd, Debra Lynn. *Nontoxic, Natural, and Earthwise*. New York: Jeremy Tarcher, 1990.

Dossey, Larry. *Healing Words*. New York: HarperSanFrancisco, 1993.

Gach, Michael Reed. *Acupressure's Potent Points*. New York: Bantam, 1990.

Gerber, Richard. Vibrational Medicine. Santa Fe: Bear and Company, 1988.

Goldberg, Burton (ed.) *Alternative Medicine: The Definitive Guide*, Tiburon, CA: Future Medicine, 1993.

Gordon, Rena, Barbara Cable Nienstedt, and Wilbert M. Gesler. *Alternative Therapies: Expanding Options in Health Care*. New York: Springer, 1998.

Hoffman, Ronald. *Seven Weeks to a Settled Stomach*. New York: Simon and Schuster, 1990.

B.K.S. Iyengar. *Light on Yoga*. New York: Schocken, 1979.

Klein, Allen. *The Healing Power of Humor*. New York: Jeremy Tarcher, 1989.

Laux, Marcus, and Christine Conrad. *Natural Woman, Natural Menopause*, New York: HarperCollins, 1997.

Lerner, Michael. *Choices in Healing*. Cambridge, MA: MIT Press, 1994.

Murray, Michael T. *Natural Alternatives to Over-the-Counter and Prescription Drugs*. New York: William Morrow, 1994.

Murray, Michael T. and Joseph Pizzorno.
    Encyclopedia of Natural Medicine. Rocklin,
    CA: Prima, 1991.

Nesse, Randolph M. and George C. Williams. *Why
    We Get Sick: The New Science of Darwinian
    Medicine*, New York: Times Books, 1994.

Ornish, Dean. *Dr. Dean Ornish's Program for
    Reversing Heart Disease*. New York: Random
    House, 1990.

Ornstein, Robert and David Sobel, *Healthy
    Pleasures*. New York: Addison Wesley, 1990.

Payer, Lynn. *Medicine and Culture*, New York:
    Henry Holt, 1988.

Payer, Lynn. *Disease Mongers*, New York:
    John Wiley, 1992.

Prevention editors. *The Doctor's Book of Home
    Remedies*. Emmaus, PA, Rodale, 1990.

Schmidt, Michael. *Healing Childhood Ear
    Infections*. Berkeley: North Atlantic, 1996.

Weil, Andrew. *Health and Healing*. Boston:
    Houghton Mifflin, 1983.

——. *Natural Health, Natural Medicine*. Boston:
    Houghton Mifflin, 1990.

Whitmont, Edward C. *The Alchemy of Healing*.
    Berkeley: North Atlantic, 1994.

NUTRITION

Balch, James F. and Phyllis A. *Prescription for Nutritional Healing*. New York: Avery, 1997.

Carper, Jean. *The Food Pharmacy*. New York: Bantam, 1988.

Davies, Stephen and Alan Stewart. *Nutritional Medicine*. New York: Avon, 1987.

Gallagher, John. *Good Health with Vitamins and Minerals*. New York: Summit, 1990.

Janson, Michael. *The Vitamin Revolution*. Greenville, NH: Arcadia, 1996.

McDougall, John A. *The McDougall Program for Women*. New York: Dutton, 1999.

Murray, Michael T. *Encyclopedia of Nutritional Supplements*. Rocklin, CA: Prima, 1996.

Null, Gary. *The Complete Guide to Sensible Eating*. New York: Four Walls Eight Windows, 1990.

Reuben, Carolyn and Joan Priestly. *Essential Supplements for Women*. New York: Pedigree, 1989.

Robbins, John. *Diet for a New America*. Walpole, NH: Stillpoint, 1987.

——. *Reclaiming Our Health*. Tiburon, CA: HJ Kramer, 1996.

HOMEOPATHIC MEDICINES

Cummings, Stephen and Dana Ullman.
*Everybody's Guide to Homeopathic
Medicines*. New York: Jeremy
Tarcher/Putnam, 1997.
Ullman, Dana. *Homeopathy A–Z*. Carlsbad, CA:
Hay House, 1999.
——, *Discovering Homeopathy: Medicine for the
21st Cen*tury. Berkeley: North Atlantic, 1991.

HERBS

Blumenthal, Mark et al. (editors). *The Complete
German Commission E Monographs*. Austin:
American Botanical Council, 1998.
Brown, Don. *Herbal Prescriptions for Better
Health*. Rocklin, CA: Prima, 1996.
Castleman, Michael. *The Healing Herbs*.
Emmaus, PA: Rodale, 1991.
McQuade Crawford, Amanda. *Herbal Remedies
for Women*. Rocklin, CA: Prima, 1997.
PDR For Herbal Medicines. Montvale, NJ:
Medical Economics, 1999.
Tierra, Michael. *The Way of Herbs*. New York:
Pocket, 1990.
Wormwood, Valerie Ann. *The Fragrant Mind*.
Novato, CA: New World Library, 1996.

MAGAZINES, NEWSLETTERS, AND JOURNALS

Alternative and Complementary Therapies,
2 Madison Ave., Larchmont, NY 10538.

Alternative Therapies in Health and Medicine,
101 Columbia, Aliso Viejo, CA 92656.

Alternative Medicine Advisor, P.O. Box 420235,
Palm Coast, FL 32142.

Dr. Andrew Weil's Self Healing, 42 Pleasant St.,
Watertown, MA 02472.

*Focus on Alternative and Complementary
Therapies* (FACT), Pharmaceutical Press,
1 Lambeth High St. London SE1 7NJ, UK.

Health Facts, 237 Thompson St., New York,
NY 10012.

Healthy Living, 1790 Broadway, 12th floor,
New York, NY 10019.

HerbalGram, P.O. Box 201660, Austin, TX
78720.

Integrative Medicine Consult, 43 Bowdoin St.,
Boston, MA 02114.

*Journal of Alternative and Complementary
Therapies*, 2 Madison Ave., Larchmont, NY
10538.

Let's Live, P.O. Box 54192, Boulder, CO 80322.

Natural Health, 70 Lincoln St., 5th floor, Boston,
MA 02111.

Townsend Letter for Doctors, 911 Tyler St.,
   Port Townsend, WA 98368.
U.C. Berkeley Wellness Letter, P.O. Box 420148,
   Palm Coast, FL 32142.
What Doctors Don't Tell You, 105 W.
   Monument St., Baltimore, MD 21201.
Yoga Journal, 2054 University Avenue, Berkeley,
   CA 94704.

ᏸᏸ

About the Author

~~~~~~~

Dana Ullman, M.P.H., is widely recognized as one of the foremost spokespersons for homeopathic medicine in the United States. He has authored six books, including *Homeopathy A-Z* (Hay House, 1999); *The Consumer's Guide to Homeopathy* (Tarcher/Putnam, 1996); and *Discovering Homeopathy: Medicine for the 21st Century* (North Atlantic, 1991), which includes a foreword by Dr. Ronald W. Davey, physician to Her Majesty Queen Elizabeth II. Dana is the President of the Foundation for Homeopathic Education and Research, an elected Board member of the National Center for Homeopathy, and directs Homeopathic Educational Services, America's largest publisher and distributor of homeopathic books, tapes, software, and medicine kits.

Dana co-taught a ten-week course on homeopathy at the University of California at San Francisco School of Medicine from 1993 to 1995 and again in 1998. He also serves as a member of the Advisory Council of the Alternative Medicine Center at Columbia

136 ☤ THE STEPS TO HEALING

University's College of Physicians and Surgeons and is a consultant to Harvard Medical School's Center to Assess Alternative Therapy for Chronic Illness.

ඖ ඖ ඖ

Dana is interested in hearing about the insights and experiences you've had after reading this book. Feel free to contact him at:

Dana Ullman, M.P.H.
2124 Kittredge St.
Berkeley, CA 94704
e-mail: **Mail@homeopathic.com**
Website: **www.homeopathic.com**

ඖඖඖ

Notes

Notes

Notes

Notes

Notes

Notes

Notes

Other Hay House Titles of Related Interest

~~~~~~~~

Aromatherapy A–Z, by Connie and Alan Higley, and Pat Leatham

Constant Craving: What Your Food Cravings Mean and How to Overcome Them, by Doreen Virtue, Ph.D.

Deep Healing: The Essence of Mind/Body Medicine, by Emmett Miller, M.D.

The Essential Flower Essence Handbook: Remedies for Inner Well-being, by Lila Devi

Heal Your Body A–Z, by Louise L. Hay

Heal Your Life with Home Remedies and Herbs, by Hanna Kroeger

Your Personality, Your Health, by Carol Ritberger, Ph.D.

☜☞

All of the above titles can be ordered through your local bookstore, or by calling Hay House at **(800) 654-5126.**

The Steps to Healing

Healing

Wisdom from the Sages,
the Rosemarys, and the Times

Dana Ullman, M.P.H.

Hay House, Inc.
Carlsbad, California • Sydney, Australia

Published and distributed in the United States by:
Hay House, Inc., P.O. Box 5100, Carlsbad, CA 92018-5100
(800) 654-5126 • (800) 650-5115 (fax)

Editorial supervision: Jill Kramer • *Design:* Jenny Richards

Portions of this work were originally published as part of the book *The One Minute or so Healer,* by Dana Ullman, published by G.P. Putnam's Sons, New York, New York, © 1991.

Library of Congress Cataloging-in-Publication Data

Ullman, Dana.
    The steps to healing : wisdom from the Sages, the Rosemarys, and the Times / Dana Ullman.
        p.   cm.
    Includes bibliographical references.
    ISBN 1-56170-657-4 (tradepaper)
    1. Homeopathy. 2. Herbs--Therapeutic use. 3. Diet therapy.
I. Title.
RX'76.U454 1999
615.5'32--dc21   99-045724
                                                             CIP

ISBN 1-56170-657-4

02   01 00 99   4 3 2 1
First Printing, November 1999

Printed in Canada